Dr David Bellamy is an internationally-renowned broadcaster and campaigner on conservation issues. A distinguished botanist and marine biologist, he has been an award-winning presenter and script writer for network television programmes worldwide. A trustee of the Living Landscape Trust, he is also Founder Director of the Conservation Foundation.

Dr Bellamy's many previous books include *England's Last Wilderness* (Michael Joseph), *Tomorrow's Earth* (Heinemann Educational), *Blooming Bellamy* (BBC Books), *Poo, You and the Potoroo's Loo* (Portland Press) and, for Frances Lincoln, the *Our Changing World* series and *How Green Are You?*

Jill Dow trained at the Royal College graduating she has worked as a freelance illustrator specialising in natural history. Her other books for Frances Lincoln are the *Windy Edge Farm* stories, and *Songbird Story*, with Michael Rosen. Jill Dow lives in Thornhill, near Stirling, with her husband and their three young children.

the
stream

the po

Apple Tree Farm

the highest point
of the track

e old track

The Roadside © Frances Lincoln Limited 1988, 1999
Text © Botanical Enterprises Publications Ltd 1988, 1999
Illustrations © Jill Dow 1988

Published in Great Britain in 1999 by
Frances Lincoln Limited, 4 Torriano Mews
Torriano Avenue, London NW5 2RZ

First published in the *Bellamy's Changing World* series
by Macdonald & Co. (Publishers) Ltd. 1988
The series has been revised and updated by David Bellamy
for this new edition.

British Library Cataloguing in Publication Data
available on request

ISBN 0-7112-1383-6

Printed in Hong Kong

1 3 5 7 9 8 6 4 2

Our Changing World

The
Roadside

David Bellamy

with illustrations by Jill Dow

FRANCES LINCOLN

It's midsummer and just off the main road, two kinds of countryside meet at this gate. In the field a crop of wheat is nearly ripe. Soon the machinery will be brought in to harvest the grain and take it away to store. The track goes on to the right and is rarely used. It leads to Apple Tree Farm, but the big company that farms the land today doesn't use the buildings. The farmhouse is deserted and the partly overgrown track is a perfect home for all sorts of wildlife. Butterflies and other insects feed on the nectar of the ox-eye daisies, chicory and purple knapweed and vetch, and a vole pokes its head out of an old can which has been carelessly thrown away.

Further on, where the old track goes through a wood, ferns and mosses nestle in the damp coolness beneath the trees and a toad sits motionless on a stone. In places the ruts have filled with water and golden kingcups and rushes grow round them. The fallen trunk of a silver birch tree is riddled

with holes made by woodpeckers
searching for insects, and clusters
of bracket fungi are growing on the
dead wood. A fox hurries away
round the corner. He has to be
careful when people are about.

Just beyond the wood the foxes have their earth under the hedgerow of sweet chestnut and dog-rose bushes. With only the cows looking on, the vixen rolls in the loose earth and the dog fox sniffs cautiously at a large toad which he has disturbed from its resting place. He knows it has a nasty taste and he'd better stick to eating rabbits, birds, rats and mice, if he can catch them. Though all is quiet here now, the foxes have to watch out for danger. A track like this is popular with people with guns.

A stream runs across the track further down and into the pond in the field beyond. The great willow tree likes the damp, so do the reedmace and the sedge growing in front of it at the edge of the water. It's very quiet today.

A fish jumps and startles the heron. The otters playing on the other side of the pond look up too. After some rain, young toads have come out to sit on the waterlily leaves, while the old toad tries in vain to catch a large dragonfly. In the reeds a pair of reed warblers are also looking for insects to eat. How safe is that damsel fly?

As the track winds up the hill again it runs close to more of the farm company's neat fields, which grow only cereals or grass. No flowers. No nectar for butterflies. A wildlife desert. But the edge by the old track is unkempt. It's overgrown with tall yellow golden rod, the pink spears of willowherb, clumps of mauve michaelmas daisies and, below them, poppies, ragwort and sunspurge. A flock of sparrows feeds on the seeds. The dog fox hunts along the far side of the field and some harvest mice have woven a nest among the barley stalks.

At the highest part of the track there is a fine view of the surrounding countryside. Most of the old hedgerows have been left. But there are tall new grain silos in the distance, big enough to hold the grain from very large fields – a sign of changes to come. Here the track passes round an outcrop of sandstone where butterflies sun their wings and banded snails cluster on nearby plants.

A thrush has been feeding, using a flat stone to smash open the shells of the snails it likes to eat. Judging by the owl pellets lying on the other stone, that tawny owl flying over the fields in the late afternoon rests here between meals. One of the pellets he coughed up has broken open. It is full of all the indigestible bits, like the fur and bones, of the mice and voles he fed on.

From round the corner where brambles, red campion and sweet cicely flank the track you can see down to the old farm at last. But far from being deserted today it seems to be a centre of activity.

At the bottom of the hill a surveyor stands with a special measuring instrument called a theodolite, ready to check

the rise of the land all the way up to another one at the top. He seems to have big changes in mind. It looks as if the peace of the old farm is about to be disturbed; already the swallows that nested in the ruined buildings are flying away, and the tawny owl's home in the dead tree may not last long either.

But what's going to happen?

By the following spring the path of the track has turned into a sea of mud. Most of the plants and creatures have disappeared and only the rushes flourish in the wheel tracks.

This is where the pond used to be. The toads, unable to find their usual spawning place, have chosen one of these puddles to lay this year's strings of eggs. But will they have a chance to hatch out? The foxes are exploring this strange new landscape too.

By the summer, despite the upheaval that continues all around, some plants and animals have made themselves at home. Today is a Sunday and all is quiet. Sparrows peck at the watchman's sandwiches when he goes into his hut, starlings perch boldly by the steps and one of the foxes even searches for titbits in the rubbish sacks. Although it's only been there a short time, the raw mound of earth is covered with new growth. Flowers like shepherd's purse, goldenrod and the bright blue cornflowers, which grow quickly from seed in the disturbed soil, attract the butterflies, and the ragwort is covered with cinnabar moth caterpillars.

At last the work is finished. So this is what it was all for!
People had campaigned to try to stop the road, but they
have lost their battle. Where the old track used to wind,
a great, straight, six-lane road is ready for the traffic. Most
of the wood is still there and the verges are seeded with
grass and summer flowers that feed the butterflies again.

The kestrel now hunts for mice and voles at the side of the
road, and at night maybe even the owl returns. Along the
central reservation the ragwort and the cranesbill with its
pointed seed capsules are flourishing. In between, ink cap
fungus has sprung up after last night's rain.

Three years have passed. It is spring again. Where the hill
once used to rise above the old farmhouse, now the road runs
through a new cutting in the sandstone. The rocky walls on
either side are already riddled with the nest holes of
sand martins. One bird is busy enlarging the hold to make
room for the baby birds which will soon hatch out.

Despite the cars roaring past only a few metres away, the vixen dozes peacefully in the sun. She knows that her cubs are safe to chase butterflies, so long as they don't stray on the road. People are not allowed to walk here any more and that means no guns. The stinging nettles don't bother the foxes either.

The peace and quiet have gone forever, and traffic fumes pollute the air. The road builders have tried their best. They have laid a pipe under the road to carry the stream to a big new pond on the other side. This also gives the toads a safe way through from their home in the woods to their mating grounds in the pond. The reed warblers may return to the pond soon, but sadly there is no sign of the otters, not even their footprints or their droppings, or of the heron. Perhaps there are no fish yet for them to eat.

The best news is that Apple Tree Farm has a new owner who is farming the organic way, without using chemicals. Now the wildlife and wildflowers will have a much greater chance of survival.

the new road

the new
pond

the
sandstone
cliff

MORE TITLES IN THE
OUR CHANGING WORLD SERIES

The Rockpool

A tale of the fascinating animal and plant life in the ever-changing world
of the rockpool, and the way they are affected by a disastrous oil spill.
ISBN 0-7112-1386-0   £4.99

The Forest

A beautifully-illustrated exploration of the animal and plant life of the forest, and
what happens when an ancient, storm-damaged oak tree is cut down.
ISBN 0-7112-1385-2 £4.99

The River

A story of the birds, fish and plants that live in and on the banks of the river,
and what happens when man threatens to destroy them.
ISBN 0-7112-1387-9   £4.99

The *Our Changing World* series is suitable for National Curriculum Science,
Key Stages 1 and 2; English – Reading, Key Stages 1 and 2
Scottish Guidelines Environmental Studies, Levels B and C;
English Language – Reading, Levels B and C

ALSO BY DAVID BELLAMY

How Green Are You?

Can you help save the world? Yes you can! Follow the Friendly Whale and learn how
you can save energy, protect wildlife and help clean up the water and the air.

Suitable for National Curriculum Science, Key Stages 1 and 2;
Geography, Key Stages 1 and 2
Scottish Guidelines Environmental Studies, Levels B and C
ISBN 0-7112-0679-1   £4.99